CONTINENTS

UNCOVERED

ASIA

KARA SEA

ARCTIC CIRCLE

URAL MOUNTAINS

LAKE BAIKAL

SEA OF OKHOTSK

AMUR RIVER

KAZAKH STEPPE

ARAL SEA

QINGHAI LAKE

MOUNT FUJI

Written by Rob Colson
Illustrated by Josy Bloggs

FRANKLIN WATTS
LONDON • SYDNEY

First published in Great Britain in 2023
by Hodder & Stoughton

Copyright © Hodder & Stoughton
Limited, 2023

Credits
Series Editor: Amy Pimperton
Series Designer: Ed Simkins
Illustrator: Josy Bloggs

HB ISBN: 978 1 4451 8096 0
PB ISBN: 978 1 4451 8097 7

Printed in Dubai

MIX
Paper from
responsible sources
FSC® C104740
FSC
www.fsc.org

Franklin Watts
An imprint of
Hachette Children's Group
Part of Hodder & Stoughton
Carmelite House
50 Victoria Embankment
London EC4Y 0DZ

An Hachette UK Company
www.hachette.co.uk
www.hachettechildrens.co.uk

The facts and statistics were
correct at the time of press.

We recommend adult supervision at
all times while doing the activities in
this book. Always be aware that craft
materials may contain allergens, so check
the packaging for allergens if there is a
risk of an allergic reaction. Anyone with
a known allergy must avoid these.
• Wear an apron and cover surfaces.
• Tie back long hair.
• Ask an adult for help with cutting
  and glueing.
• Check materials for allergens.

CONTENTS

WHERE IN THE WORLD?

Asia is the largest continent in the world. It forms part of a larger landmass called Eurasia, which it shares with the continent of Europe. It sits almost entirely in the Northern Hemisphere, stretching from the Ural Mountains in the west to the Chukchi Peninsula in the east. The largest country by area in Asia is Russia, part of which is in Europe. Between them, China and India are home to more than one-third of the world's population.

ASIA

PACIFIC OCEAN

INDIAN OCEAN

N W E S

POLITICAL MAP

PHYSICAL MAP

Map makers create maps that show different types of information. Political maps, such as the map of Asia far left, show human features such as countries. Physical maps show the geographical features of a region, such as elevation. In the physical map of Asia to the left, high ground is shown in brown, while low ground is coloured green.

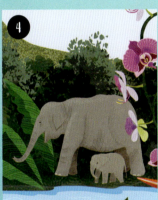

HABITATS

A habitat is an area that is home to a particular group of plants and animals. The continent of Asia contains a huge range of habitats. The north of the continent is covered by the vast taiga (1), while Central Asia is dominated by harsh deserts, such as the Gobi Desert (2). Conditions are also hard in the Himalayas (3), the highest mountain range in the world. Further south, the island of Borneo straddles the Equator. Borneo is warm and wet all year long and covered in lush rainforest (4).

FACTS

• Area: 44.6 million square kilometres

• Major rivers: Yangtze, Yellow, Ganges, Li, Mekong, Indus, Brahmaputra, Euphrates, Amur

• Highest peak: Mount Everest, Himalayas, 8,849 metres

• Major mountain ranges: Himalayas, Karakoram, Zagros, Urals, Pamir Mountains, Caucasus

CENTRAL AND EAST ASIA

The habitats of Central and East Asia range from Arctic tundra in the north to lush rainforests in the south. The Eurasian Steppe is a huge area of grassland in Central Asia, while coniferous forests dominate much of Siberia. The two longest rivers in Asia, the Yangtze and Yellow rivers, both flow from west to east through China.

KAZAKH STEPPE

The Kazakh Steppe, part of the Eurasian Steppe, is a dry, grassy plain with a harsh climate. Few trees grow there due to low rainfall. For nearly half the year, temperatures rarely rise above 0°C, while the short summer is very hot. Strong winds blow all year long. The animals of the Kazakh Steppe include herds of saiga antelope, which migrate long distances across the plain in search of fresh grass to eat.

KARA SEA

URAL MOUNTAINS

KAZAKH STEPPE

ARAL SEA

BLACK SEA

CASPIAN SEA

HIMALAYAS

TIBETAN PLATEAU

About five times the size of France, the Tibetan Plateau is the biggest plateau in the world. It extends north from the Himalaya Mountains. The average height of the plateau is more than 4,500 metres. Much of the land is covered in tundra-like grasslands.

LAPTEV SEA

ARCTIC CIRCLE

BERING SEA

LAKE BAIKAL

AMUR RIVER

SEA OF OKHOTSK

YANGTZE RIVER

The Yangtze River is the longest river in Asia and the largest river to flow entirely within one country. It stretches for 6,300 kilometres across China from Tibet in the west to the East China Sea in the east. Along the way, the river passes through many different habitats, including steep mountains, dense forests and fertile wetlands. The Three Gorges Dam on the Yangtze was completed in 2012. The dam is the world's largest power station, generating electricity for much of central China.

NGHAI LAKE

TIBETAN PLATEAU

YELLOW RIVER

MOUNT FUJI

EAST CHINA SEA

YANGTZE RIVER

SIBERIAN TAIGA

Also known as snow forest, taiga is a habitat made up mostly of coniferous trees. The Siberian taiga is one of the largest forests in the world, covering 12 million square kilometres. Snow covers the ground for most of the year. When it melts, the taiga springs to life during the short summer. Flowers bloom and animals such as brown bears eat as much as they can to fatten themselves up for the coming winter.

RED SQUIRREL

CONIFERS

Conifers are trees such as pines that produce seeds inside a protective cone. Their needle-like leaves have a waxy coating that stops the leaves from losing water. This helps the tree to survive the harsh Siberian winter. A variety of animals feed on the cones of Siberian conifers, including the Siberian flying squirrel, which glides from tree to tree using a flap of skin that stretches between its front and rear legs.

SIBERIAN FLYING SQUIRREL

FACTS

SIBERIAN TAIGA

• Weighing in at up to 300 kilogrammes, Siberian tigers are the largest tigers in the world. They hunt a range of animals including deer and wild boar. Only about 500 Siberian tigers remain in the wild.

• Wolverines are fierce predators that range over huge areas in search of food. Although they are capable of killing prey much larger than themselves, wolverines mostly feed on carrion (dead animals).

SIBERIAN MUSK

SIBERIAN CHIPMUNK

GREAT
GREY OWL

GREY WOLF

BROWN BEAR

LEMMING

Pinecone hygrometer

Pinecones open when the air is dry and close when it is moist. Make a pinecone hygrometer and use it to measure the humidity (amount of water) in the air.

Monday = Dry

1. With the help of an adult, glue a pinecone to a piece of cardboard and glue a toothpick to the end of one of the scales. This will be your pointer.

2. Use a protractor to draw a curved scale around either side of the pointer.

3. Record the position of the pointer every day for a week. Does it go down during dry weather and up when it is raining?

LI RIVER

LI RIVER

The Li River in China flows through a beautiful landscape of towering hills with nearly vertical slopes. Between the river and the hills, farmers grow rice in spiralling, terraced paddy fields. With a warm and wet subtropical climate, this region is home to a diverse range of plants and animals.

• Growing up to 1.8 metres long, the South China giant salamander is the biggest amphibian in the world. It lives in rocky streams, feeding on insects, frogs, fish and other salamanders!

• Local fishermen have traditionally caught fish in the Li River with the help of specially trained cormorants. The birds dive into the water from a bamboo raft and return with a mouthful of fish.

CHINESE EGRET

CORMORANT

OSMANTHUS TREE

BUFFALO

ERODED HILLS

PIT VIPER

The rugged landscape of the Li River valley has been created by millions of years of erosion. The rocks around the river are made of limestone. This soft rock dissolves in water and is easily worn away by rivers and streams. This erosion has created hills with strange shapes that sometimes resemble animals, including one that is known as Elephant Trunk Hill.

ACTIVITY

Acid erosion

The mountain streams around the Li River erode limestone rock because the water is slightly acidic. Watch how acidic vinegar can destroy a stick of chalk.

1. With the help of an adult, place a stick of chalk in a clear glass and pour vinegar over it. Place the glass in a safe place.

2. Check on the chalk every day for the next few days and note how the chalk changes. Do you notice sediment building up at the bottom of the glass? How long does it take for the stick to disappear completely?

SNUB-NOSED MONKEY

CHINESE POND HERON

GOLDEN
EAGLE

GOBI DESERT

The Gobi Desert is a vast, cold desert that stretches for more than 1,600 kilometres across northern China and southern Mongolia. In many parts of the Gobi Desert, temperatures can reach as high as 30°C during the day before plunging to below 0°C at night. The plants and animals that live here need to be tough to survive these extreme swings in temperature.

JERBOA

Hopping along on its hind legs, the jerboa looks like a miniature kangaroo. This small rodent has huge ears so it can listen out for predators, such as eagles. It can leap 3 metres high and run at speeds of up to 25 kilometres per hour when it is chased. It generally shelters in a burrow during the day, emerging at dusk to feed on plants and insects.

FACTS

GOBI
DESERT

• The Gobi pit viper is a snake that feeds on rodents, lizards and frogs. Heat-sensing pits on its head help the viper to detect the body warmth of its prey.

• The golden eagle soars across the Gobi keeping a sharp eye out for its favourite prey, the jerboa.

MARBLED
POLECAT

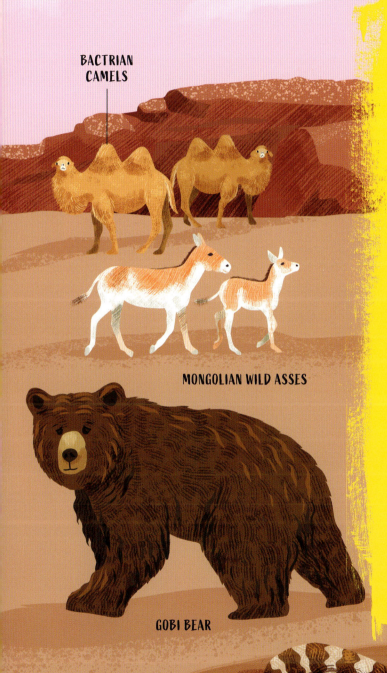

BACTRIAN CAMELS

MONGOLIAN WILD ASSES

GOBI BEAR

PIT VIPER

Sound cone

Jerboas have huge ears to help them to hear quiet sounds. Make a simple sound cone to turn up the volume on the sounds around you.

1. Roll a large sheet of thin cardboard or posterboard into a cone shape. Leave a small hole about 1 cm across at the pointed end and make the wide end as big as possible. Tape the edge into position.

2. Now try out your sound cone. Hold the small end to your ear and see what you can hear. Make sure you don't push the cone into your ear.

LAKE BAIKAL

Lake Baikal in Russia is the deepest lake in the world. Plunging to a depth of 1,642 metres, the lake holds more freshwater than all the Great Lakes of North America combined. More than 2,000 species of plant and animal live in Lake Baikal, and most of them are found nowhere else in the world. For several months each winter, the lake completely freezes over.

FACTS

LAKE BAIKAL ★

• More than 50 species of fish live in the clear waters of Lake Baikal, including the omul, a whitefish that is considered a great delicacy in Russia.

• Flatworms up to 30 centimetres long move around the bottom of the lake in search of prey. More than 140 different species of flatworm are unique to Lake Baikal.

CASPIAN TERN

NERPA

The Baikal seal, or nerpa, is the only freshwater seal in the world. It can hold its breath for nearly an hour as it dives to depths of up to 300 metres in search of fish. During winter, the seals use their strong claws to cut holes in the ice, which can be up to 2 metres thick. They dive for fish under the ice, coming up to breathe at the holes they have made.

EURASIAN BROWN BEAR

BAIKAL TEAL

Increasing pressure

At the bottom of Lake Baikal, the water pressure is so great that a human would be crushed by it. See how water pressure increases with depth with this simple experiment.

1. Ask an adult to cut a series of small holes in the side of a 2-litre plastic bottle. Cut three or four in a line from top to bottom, about 5 cm apart.

2. Hold the bottle over the sink and fill it with water. Watch how the water is pushed out of the holes into the sink and down the plug hole. The lower the hole, the further the jet of water will be pushed out.

WHITE-TAILED EAGLE

ELK

RED FOX

MOUNTAIN HARE

SOUTHEAST ASIA

Southeast Asia is mostly warm and wet, but the rains in much of the region are highly seasonal. There are more than 25,000 islands in Southeast Asia. The southernmost islands of the region cross the Equator to lie in the Southern Hemisphere.

MONSOON SEASON

Every summer in South Asia, a change in the wind direction means the start of the monsoon season. The air above land heats up more quickly than the air above the ocean. This causes a wind to blow from the sea to the land, bringing with it lots of moisture, which falls as torrential rain. The summer monsoon accounts for about 80 per cent of annual rainfall, filling up the wells and aquifers that provide water supplies for the rest of the year.

MEKONG RIVER

ANDAMAN SEA

GULF OF THAILAND

SO...

EQUATOR

JAVA SEA

MEKONG RIVER

The Mekong River flows south from the Tibetan Plateau, passing through six countries to empty into the South China Sea in Vietnam. The Mekong is home to more species of large fish than any other river in the world, including the Mekong giant catfish, which can grow up to 3 metres long. Other large animals found in the river include the Asian giant softshell turtle and the Irrawaddy dolphin.

TUBBATAHA NATIONAL PARK

The Tubbataha National Park is a protected region in the Sulu Sea in the Philippines that contains a number of uninhabited islands, lagoons and coral reefs. The reefs are home to more than 600 species of fish, including sharks, manta rays, lionfish and clownfish. Dolphins, whales and sea turtles are also found there. Located 150 kilometres from the nearest inhabited island, the park is protected from illegal fishing by a team of park rangers.

PHILIPPINE SEA

TUBBATAHA NATIONAL PARK

SULU SEA

CELEBES SEA

BANDA SEA

FLORES SEA

ARAFURA SEA

TIMOR SEA

BISMARCK SEA

N
W   E
S

WREATHED
HORNBILL

BORNEO RAINFOREST

Straddling the Equator, much of the island of Borneo is covered in the thickest rainforest. More than 10,000 species of plant grow on Borneo, including 3,000 different species of tree. A wide variety of birds and mammals make their home in the forest.

FACTS

BORNEO
RAINFOREST

ORCHID

BORNEO
ELEPHANTS

• More than 2,000 different kinds of orchid grow on Borneo. Each year, the orchids grow beautiful flowers to attract birds and bees.

• The corpse flower plant grows the largest flowers in the world, measuring 1 metre across. The stinky flowers smell of rotting meat to attract insects.

BORNEO
KINGFISHER

CORPSE FLOWER

MACAQUE

ORANGUTAN

Orangutans swing through the trees with their long, powerful arms and hook-shaped hands and feet. They sleep high up in carefully constructed nests, pulling together larger branches, then arranging smaller, leafy branches to make a 'mattress' and 'pillow' to curl up on. They cover themselves using leafy branches as a blanket.

SUN BEAR

MONITOR LIZARD

Paper flower

A huge range of beautiful flowers grow on Borneo. Make a colourful tissue paper flower of your own.

1. Place two sheets of tissue paper one on top of the other. Fold in half, then fold again.

2. Find the corner with separate sheets and no fold. Fold this corner to the opposite edge to make a triangle and, with an adult's help, use scissors to cut off any extra rectangle. Open the triangle up to make a square and trim off each edge with a fold to make eight separate squares.

3. Fold the eight squares in an accordion manner, making six or seven folds.

4. With an adult's help, use a stapler to staple the accordions in the centre. With the help of an adult, use scissors to round off the ends of the paper.

5. Carefully separate the layers at one end and fluff the layers to open up your flower.

KAVIR NATIONAL PARK

The Kavir National Park is a protected nature reserve in northern Iran. It is sometimes known as 'Little Africa' due to its safari-like wildlife, which includes gazelles, goats, hyenas, leopards and cheetahs. Thorny trees and bushes grow in this dry habitat, which sits at the western end of the Great Salt Desert.

WEST ASIA AND THE INDIAN SUBCONTINENT

Asia is home to the 100 highest mountains in the world. These are all found in the Himalayas or Karakoram mountains. The Indian subcontinent extends south from the Himalayas into the Indian Ocean. To the west, the Zagros Mountains stretch across Iran, Iraq and Turkey. To the south of these mountains is Mesopotamia, a fertile region around the rivers Tigris and Euphrates. Further west, the Arabian Peninsula is hot and dry.

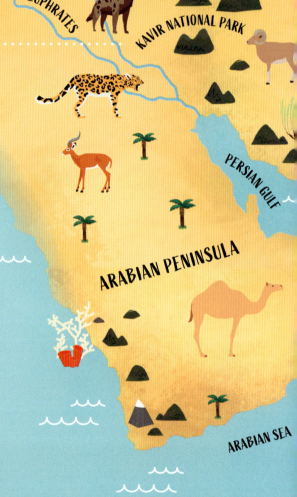

CASPIAN SEA

TIGRIS

EUPHRATES

KAVIR NATIONAL PARK

PERSIAN GULF

ARABIAN PENINSULA

ARABIAN SEA

HIGHS & LOWS

DRIEST PLACE:
ADEN, YEMEN, 45.7 MILLIMETRES OF RAIN PER YEAR

RECORD HIGH TEMPERATURE: 54°C, TIRAT ZVI, ISRAEL

KAPLANKYR RESERVE

RIVER GANGES

The River Ganges rises in the Himalaya Mountains and crosses northern India to flow into the Bay of Bengal in Bangladesh. It is the third-largest river in the world in terms of discharge. The river is home to the rare gharial (a kind of crocodile) and the even rarer South Asian river dolphin, both of which feed on the river's fish. The Ganges is also crucial to the lives of the many millions of people who live alongside it.

GREAT SALT DESERT

INDUS RIVER

GULF OF OMAN

RIVER GANGES

SRI LANKAN RAINFOREST

BAY OF BENGAL

ANDAMAN SEA

SRI LANKAN RAINFOREST

LACCADIVE SEA

The tropical island of Sri Lanka is covered in thick forests. Many of the plants and animals found here are unique to the island. These include the red slender loris, a small primate found only in the rainforests of south-west Sri Lanka. This nocturnal creature has huge, bulging eyes, which help it to see in the dark. Lorises sleep in groups in the trees during the day. At night, they split up to forage for insects.

N W E S

EQUATOR

THE SUNDARBANS

The Sundarbans is a tidal area around the Ganges Delta in Bangladesh. This is the place where three great rivers – the Ganges, the Brahmaputra and the Meghna – come together to drain into the ocean. The vast swamplands of the delta contain the largest mangrove forests in the world. Mangroves are trees that grow in tidal areas that are regularly washed by saltwater.

FACTS

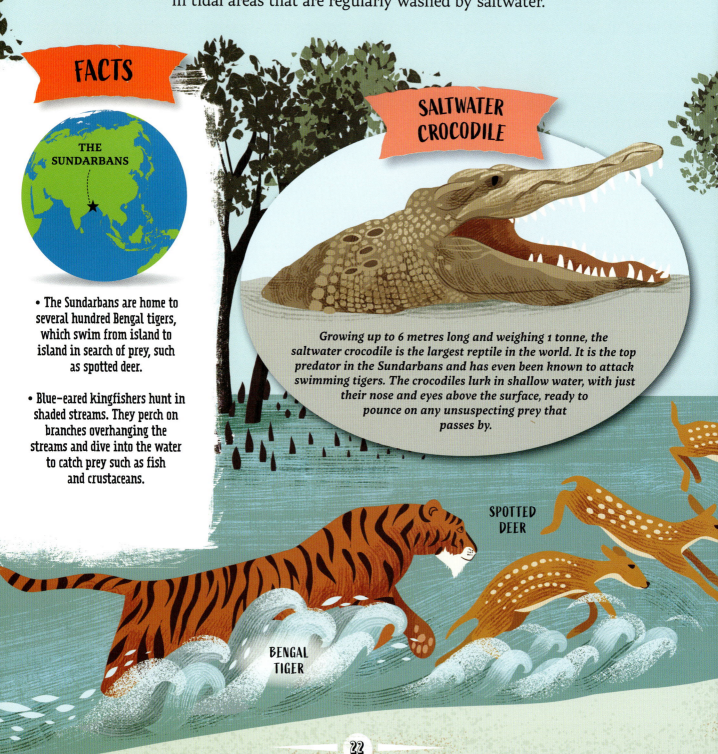

THE SUNDARBANS

- The Sundarbans are home to several hundred Bengal tigers, which swim from island to island in search of prey, such as spotted deer.

- Blue-eared kingfishers hunt in shaded streams. They perch on branches overhanging the streams and dive into the water to catch prey such as fish and crustaceans.

SALTWATER CROCODILE

Growing up to 6 metres long and weighing 1 tonne, the saltwater crocodile is the largest reptile in the world. It is the top predator in the Sundarbans and has even been known to attack swimming tigers. The crocodiles lurk in shallow water, with just their nose and eyes above the surface, ready to pounce on any unsuspecting prey that passes by.

SPOTTED DEER

BENGAL TIGER

BLUE-EARED
KINGFISHER

RHESUS
MACAQUE

KING COBRA

Salt water

At tidal deltas, such as the Ganges delta, fresh water from rivers meets salt water from the ocean. Try this experiment to see how salt water is more dense than fresh water.

1. Ask an adult to help with this activity. Half fill a clear plastic cup with water from the tap and add two tablespoons of salt water. Stir until all the salt is dissolved.

2. Place an ice cube on top of the salt water and leave it for about five minutes until the ice has melted. Now add a couple of drops of food colouring and watch how it disperses.

Salt water is more dense than fresh water so the melted ice forms a layer of fresh water on top of the salt water. The food colouring disperses quickly through the fresh water and takes much longer to spread into the salt water beneath it.

THE HIMALAYAS

The Himalayas are a mountain range sandwiched between the plains of Northern India and the Tibetan Plateau. Many of the world's highest mountains are found in the Himalayas, including the highest of all, Mount Everest. The Himalayas formed when the Indian continental plate pushed up against the Eurasian plate. The peaks are still slowly rising, growing by more than 1 centimetre each year.

FACTS

THE HIMALAYAS

• The Sherpa people live in the high mountains of Nepal and Tibet. Traditionally farmers and traders, in recent years many Sherpas have found work as mountain guides, and they are famed for their climbing skills.

• Living at heights of up to 5,500 metres, the snow leopard hunts mountain sheep and goats, often chasing them down the steep slopes.

HIMALAYAN BLUE SHEEP (BHARAL)

SNOW LEOPARD

RHODODENDRON

RED PANDA

YAKS

Farmers in the Himalayas keep herds of yak. They are a large kind of cattle specially adapted to the tough life high in the mountains. Yaks have thick fur, layers of insulating fat and large lungs and heart. These animals are farmed for their meat and milk, and also used to carry goods across mountain passes.
In Tibet, yak races are held during festivals through the year.

Fold mountains

The Himalayas are fold mountains, formed as Earth's continental plates push against one another. Create a fold mountain range using towels and see how the layers crumple.

1. Find four or five colourful towels and place them flat in a pile on a table, with contrasting colours next to one another.

2. Stack books on either side of the towels. These will be your continental plates.

3. With a friend, slowly push the books towards one another. What happens to the towel layers? When fold mountain ranges are formed, the layers of rock are folded in a similar way.

HIMALAYAN TAHR

HIMALAYAN PIKA

PEOPLE AND PLACES

Asia is home to more than 4.5 billion people – more than half the world's population. The countries of Asia vary hugely in their cultures. About two-thirds of all Asians live in the continent's two largest countries, China and India.

CHINA

With a rich history dating back more than 4,000 years, China is a nation of huge contrasts, with remote rural areas and huge cities. More than 60 per cent of the population live in urban areas, and there are 20 cities with more than 5 million people. The biggest festival in the country is Chinese New Year, which falls between 20 January and 20 February. Millions of people leave the cities to welcome in the new year in their hometowns in the countryside.

MONGOLIA

CHINA

Kashgar

New Delhi

Chengdu

Lhasa

INDIA

MYANMAR (BURMA)

Naypyidaw

THAILAND

Bangkok

ANDAMAN AND NICOBAR ISLANDS

Colombo

SRI LANKA

SUMATRA

N W E S

INDIAN OCEAN

RUSSIA

Ulaanbaatar

SHANGHAI

Beijing

Xi'an

Shanghai

NORTH KOREA
Pyongyang

SOUTH KOREA
Seoul

JAPAN

Tokyo

Shanghai is China's largest city and its main business centre. Home to 25 million people, Shanghai has grown enormously in recent years as China's economy has boomed. It boasts a growing number of gleaming skyscrapers, including Shanghai Tower. Opened in 2015, the tower contains a lift that moves at 20 metres per second, reaching the top of the 632-metre-high building in under a minute.

CHINA

AREA: 9.6 MILLION SQUARE KILOMETRES

POPULATION: OVER 1.4 BILLION

MAIN LANGUAGE: STANDARD CHINESE

CAPITAL CITY: BEIJING

Taipei
City

Hong Kong

TAIWAN

VIETNAM

Hanoi

LAOS
Vientiane

CAMBODIA
Phnom Penh

Ho Chi
Minh City

PHILIPPINES
Manila

PALAWAN

MALAYSIA
Kuala Lumpur

BRUNEI

SARAWAK

SINGAPORE

BORNEO

INDONESIA

Indonesia is a large country spread across more than 17,000 islands in Southeast Asia. Java, the world's most populous island, is home to more than half of Indonesia's 270 million people. It is a culturally diverse country, and more than 700 different languages are spoken. Although most Indonesians are Muslim, a wide range of religions are practised. Borobudur on Java is the largest Buddhist temple in the world. This huge stone building is decorated with more than 500 statues of Buddha.

SULAWESI

NORTH
MALUKU

NEW GUINEA

BURU

MALUKU

PAPUA
Jayapura

Jakarta

INDONESIA

JAVA

BALI

TIMOR-LESTE

TIMOR

PEOPLE AND PLACES

The cultures of western, central and southern Asia reflect the different religions of the region. In Turkey, Iran, Afghanistan, Pakistan and a number of Arab countries, Islam is the dominant religion. Israel is a Jewish state, while South Asia covers a mix of many different faiths, including Hinduism, Buddhism and Islam.

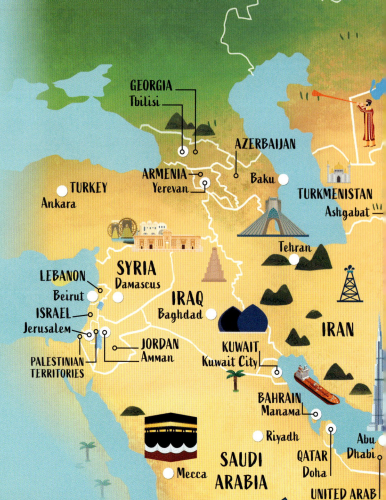

GEORGIA
Tbilisi

AZERBAIJAN

ARMENIA
Yerevan

Baku

TURKEY
Ankara

TURKMENISTAN
Ashgabat

Tehran

SYRIA
Damascus

LEBANON
Beirut

IRAQ
Baghdad

ISRAEL
Jerusalem

IRAN

JORDAN
Amman

KUWAIT
Kuwait City

PALESTINIAN
TERRITORIES

BAHRAIN
Manama

Riyadh

Abu
Dhabi

SAUDI
ARABIA

QATAR
Doha

Mecca

UNITED ARAB
EMIRATES

YEMEN

Sana'a

SAUDI ARABIA

The country of Saudi Arabia occupies most of the Arabian Peninsula in western Asia. Vast areas of the country are covered in sandy desert, including the Rub' al Khali (Empty Quarter), an area the size of France that is completely uninhabited. The Bedouin of Arabia were traditionally nomads, but today most of Saudi Arabia's people live in cities. Millions of Muslims undertake the pilgrimage known as the Hajj each year to the Saudi city of Mecca.

HIGHS & LOWS

WETTEST PLACE:
IN CHERRAPUNJI, INDIA, ON AVERAGE MORE THAN 2,500 MILLIMETRES OF RAIN FALLS EVERY JUNE.

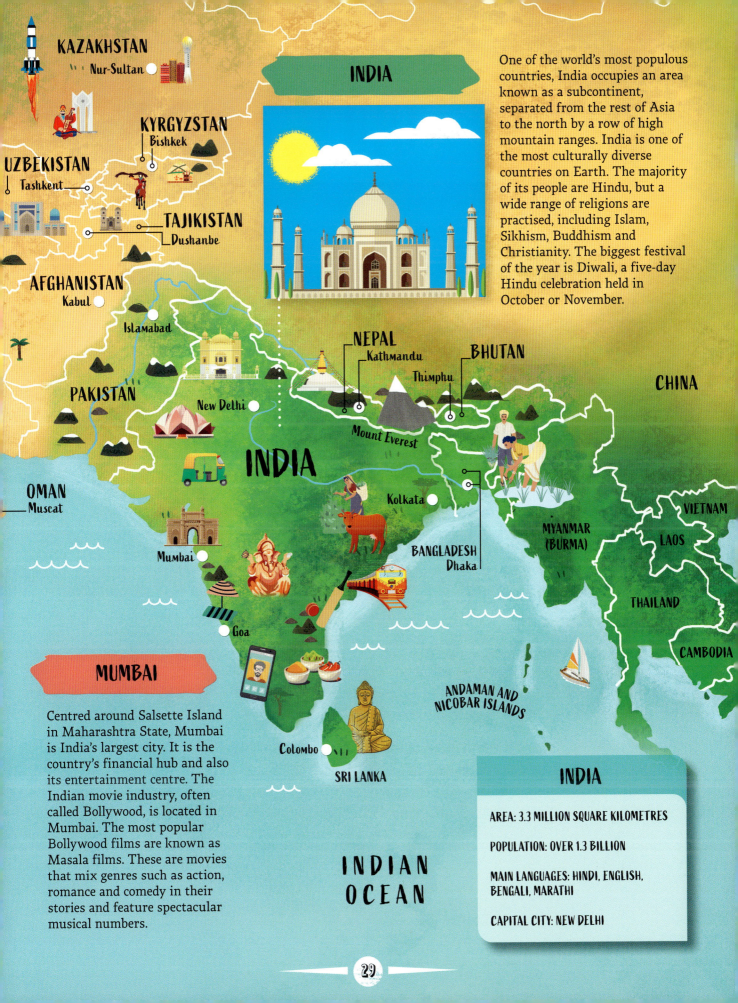

INDIA

One of the world's most populous countries, India occupies an area known as a subcontinent, separated from the rest of Asia to the north by a row of high mountain ranges. India is one of the most culturally diverse countries on Earth. The majority of its people are Hindu, but a wide range of religions are practised, including Islam, Sikhism, Buddhism and Christianity. The biggest festival of the year is Diwali, a five-day Hindu celebration held in October or November.

KAZAKHSTAN
Nur-Sultan

KYRGYZSTAN
Bishkek

UZBEKISTAN
Tashkent

TAJIKISTAN
Dushanbe

AFGHANISTAN
Kabul

Islamabad

PAKISTAN

New Delhi

NEPAL
Kathmandu

BHUTAN
Thimphu

CHINA

Mount Everest

INDIA

OMAN
Muscat

Mumbai

Kolkata

BANGLADESH
Dhaka

MYANMAR
(BURMA)

VIETNAM

LAOS

THAILAND

CAMBODIA

Goa

ANDAMAN AND
NICOBAR ISLANDS

MUMBAI

Centred around Salsette Island in Maharashtra State, Mumbai is India's largest city. It is the country's financial hub and also its entertainment centre. The Indian movie industry, often called Bollywood, is located in Mumbai. The most popular Bollywood films are known as Masala films. These are movies that mix genres such as action, romance and comedy in their stories and feature spectacular musical numbers.

Colombo

SRI LANKA

INDIAN OCEAN

INDIA

AREA: 3.3 MILLION SQUARE KILOMETRES

POPULATION: OVER 1.3 BILLION

MAIN LANGUAGES: HINDI, ENGLISH, BENGALI, MARATHI

CAPITAL CITY: NEW DELHI

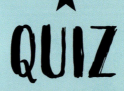

QUIZ

1. The Three Gorges Dam is built across which river in China?

2. Fishermen on the Li River train which birds to help them catch fish?

3. The deepest lake in the world, Lake Baikal, is found in which country?

4. What is the name of the torrential rains that fall every summer in South Asia?

5. How does the corpse flower attract insects?

6. What is the name of the tree-dwelling ape found in the rainforests of Borneo?

7. What is the name of the nature reserve in northern Iran that is sometimes called 'Little Africa'?

8. The Ganges Delta is located in which country?

9. Growing up to 6 metres long, which predator is the world's largest reptile?

10. Mount Everest, the highest mountain in the world, is found in which mountain range?

11. What is the name of China's largest city, which has a population of 25 million people?

12. What is the popular name for the movie industry that is based in the Indian city of Mumbai?

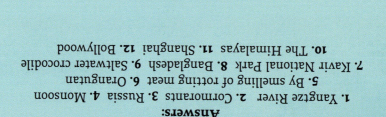

GLOSSARY

Aquifer
A layer of rock underground that contains and transmits water.

Coniferous forest
A forest made up of evergreen trees that bear cones, such as pines, spruce and fir.

Continental plates
Large pieces of Earth's crust that form the continents. The plates slowly rub against one another.

Coral reefs
Stony structures found in shallow tropical seas, built from the skeletons of tiny animals called polyps. A rich variety of creatures live in coral reefs.

Delta
A flat, fan-shaped area of land created where a river splits into many different branches and deposits sediment.

Equator
An imaginary line around Earth that is the same distance from both the North and South Poles. The Equator divides the planet into the Northern Hemisphere and the Southern Hemisphere.

Habitat
An area with the right conditions for a particular set of plants, animals and other living things to live. Those conditions may include soil type, rainfall or temperature.

Lagoon
A shallow body of salt water that is separated from the ocean by a narrow strip of land.

Paddy field
A flooded area of land used to grow rice.

Plateau
(Plural: plateaux) An area of high, flat ground.

Primates
A group of mammals that have flexible hands and large brains. The primates include monkeys, lorises and apes.

Rainforest
A dense forest rich in life that grows in areas with plentiful rainfall all year around.

Rodents
A group of mammals with front teeth that grow continuously to allow them to gnaw on objects.

Species
A group of closely related living things that reproduce with one another.

Tundra
A flat, treeless region in the far north of the continents of Asia, Europe and North America. Tundra is covered in snow for much of the year, and the subsoil remains permanently frozen.

INDEX